THE FOODIES' AND SCOFFERS' BIBLE

Culinary Confessions & Tasty Trivia From Around The World

THE FOODIES' AND SCOFFERS' BIBLE

Culinary Confessions & Tasty Trivia From Around The World

By Ruth Graham   Cartoons by Gill Toft

www.knowthescorebooks.com

Know The Score Books Limited
118 Alcester Road
Studley
Warwickshire
B80 7NT
01527 454482
info@knowthescorebooks.com

A CIP catalogue record is available for this book from the British Library   ISBN: 978-1-905449-22-4

Jacket and book design by Lisa David
Cartoons by Gill Toft

Printed and bound in Great Britain by Martins The Printer

Dedication

To my friend Nita, who still believes that if you chew and swallow fast enough, it won't count.

To Darren Hodson – thanks SO much for your endless supply of contacts and great stories. You do make me laugh!

To Liz Pimley. Your endless quest for new and interesting grains is inspiring.

And last (but definitely not least) to Liz Lebreuilly . Thanks for feeding me whilst I was too busy getting the Bible series done to do it myself. Your roasts are the business!!

~ Ruth Graham

THE FOODIES' AND SCOFFERS' BIBLE

Food glorious food! Never has there been so much choice, controversy, knowledge ignorance and interest. Every day 250,000 more consumers join the planet, but what goes into their mouth throughout their lifetime will be dictated by a mixture of tradition, information, peer-pressure, availability, technological advances, climate change and economics.

Whatever your thoughts on food, whether you live to eat or eat to live, turn the page and get your teeth into some of the most interesting, shocking and hilarious food trivia you'll ever be served.

CONTENTS

WHO SAYS WHAT ABOUT FOOD?

'Mosquitoes remind us that we are not as high up on the food chain as we think.' – Tom Wilson, actor/comedian

Culinary Quotes

I believe that if ever I had to practice cannibalism, I might manage if there were enough tarragon around.

~ **James Beard** (food author 1903-1985)

Never eat more than you can lift.

~ **Miss Piggy**

We have good days and bad days in cooking... and when you've had a bad day, when you've had 25 vegetarians walk in unannounced, this is a song that puts it all into context.

~ **Vegetarian-hating chef Gordon Ramsay**
(choosing 'Sing' by Travis, on BBC Radio 4's Desert Island Discs)

I don't like to eat snails. I prefer fast food.

~ **Roger von Oech** (*A*
Kick in the Seat of the Pants, 1996)

Escargot — nobody is sure how this got started. Probably a couple of French master chefs were standing around one day, and they found a snail, and one of them said: 'I bet that if we called this something like escargot, tourists would eat it.' They then had a hearty laugh, because 'escargot' is the French word for 'fat crawling bag of phlegm.'

~ **Dave Barry** (*Dave*
Barry's Only Travel Guide You'll Ever Need, 1991)

Come quickly! I am tasting stars.

~ **Dom Perignon**
(*1638-1714, on tasting his first sip of champagne*)

It would be nice if the Food and Drug Administration stopped issuing warnings about toxic substances and just gave me the names of one or two things still safe to eat.

~ **Robert Fuoss**
(Executive Editor, Saturday Evening Post, 1956-61)

Food critic Giles Coren, when asked 'who is the most influential chef of our time?' replied, 'Ronald McDonald, the poisonous criminal bastard.'

A food is not necessarily essential just because your child hates it.

~ **Katherine Whitehorn**
(writer/journalist)

High-tech tomatoes. Mysterious milk. Supersquash. Are we supposed to eat this stuff? Or is it going to eat us?

~ **Annita Manning**
(reporter)

My doctor told me to stop having intimate dinners for four. Unless there are three other people.

~ **Orson Welles**

Anybody who believes that the way to a man's heart is through his stomach, flunked geography.

~ Robert Byrne
(author)

A nickel will get you on the subway, but garlic will get you a seat.

~ Old New York Proverb

We are living in a world today where lemonade is made from artificial flavors and furniture polish is made from real lemons.

~ **Alfred E. Newman**
(author)

There is one thing more exasperating than a wife who can cook and won't, and that's a wife who can't cook and will.

~ **Robert Frost** (poet)

In victory you deserve champagne, in defeat you need it.

~ Napoleon Bonaparte

I cook with wine. I sometimes even add it to the food.

~ W.C. Fields
(in ' Never Give A Sucker An Even Break')

GLOBAL GUZZLING

Who eats what and where?

- The French consume over 500,000,000 snails per year.

- Yak butter is part of a Tibetan's staple diet, and they drink around 40 cups of buttered tea per day.

- In an average lifetime, the average UK citizen will consume:

  15,951 pints of milk per person
  1,200 chickens
  13,345 eggs
  2,327 kilos of potatoes
  4,283 loaves
  5,272 apples
  10,866 carrots

- Over 1,000 litres of beer are drunk in the House of Commons each week

- Quite forgetting that sweets, by definition, should taste sweet, sweet lovers in Holland and Sweden cannot get enough salt liquorice!

- The average Cruise Liner (carrying 2,500 people) would order in the following amounts every week:

24,236 pounds of beef
5,040 pounds of lamb
7,216 pounds of pork
4,600 pounds of veal
1,680 pounds of sausage
10,211 pounds of chicken
3,156 pounds of turkey
13,851 pounds of fish
350 pounds of crab
2,100 pounds of lobster
25,736 pounds of fresh vegetables
15,150 pounds of potatoes
20,003 pounds of fresh fruit
3,260 gallons of milk
1976 quarts of cream
600 gallons of ice cream
9,235 dozen eggs
5,750 pounds of sugar
3,800 pounds of rice
1,750 pounds of cereal
450 pounds of jelly

2,458 pounds of coffee
1,936 pounds of cookies
2,450 tea bags
120 pounds (54 kg) of herbs and spices
3,400 bottles of assorted wines
200 bottles of champane
200 bottles of gin
290 bottles of vodka
350 bottles of whiskey
150 bottles of rum
45 bottles of sherry
600 bottles of assorted liqueurs
10,100 bottles/cans of beer

The figures include all supplies for cooking meals in three restaurants and all nightly buffets, room service, bars and lounges, as well as all baking and confectionery supplies.
This is comparable to the provisions that any small town might consume in a week.

And on a more bizarre note....

- In May 2007 a woman in Can Tho City in China was admitted to hospital complaining of stomach ache. She was found to have 119 three-inch rusty nails in her stomach, but amazingly had just a few scratches!

- When a Swiss housewife decided to handwash the net curtains, the last thing she expected was that they would decompose into a white creamy paste in the bowl, right before her very eyes. Worried that her husband would not believe her, she left them in the bowl as proof, and popped out to the shops to purchase some new ones. Unfortunately, her husband got home early, and she came through the door to be greeted with his moans of 'Valerie – no matter how much salt and pepper I put on, this cream cheese still tastes insipid.'

- Back in the 1960s, *The Guardian* reported that laboratory tests confirmed how, after eating a curry, a shorthand-typist excreted a form of dye through her skin which turned everything she touched pink. Apparently something in her system reacted against turmeric.

FOOD FADS AND TRENDS

The 70s icon hostess trolley came into its own as a makeshift stretcher for Robert during a bout of anaphlactic shock – the trendiest food allergy of the 1990s.

British Dining Through The Decades

The trends, the people, the food. How much of this can you remember?

1960s

New tastes: **Expanding foreign communities introduced dishes like Indian and Chinese.**

Favourite Catchphrase: **'I'm not eating that foreign muck.'**

Sophisticated Dishes: **Travel made Spag Bol the height of sophistication.**

Old Favourites: **Fish and chips was still no. 1 – (even Harrods had its own-label frozen brand!)**

Consumption: **Meat and sugar were consumed at record levels. Tinned foods were the main convenience food, and white sliced bread was king.**

Hot in the kitchen: **Fanny Craddock (who, incredibly used to cook in full evening dress) was popular, assisted by husband Johnny. Male chef Graham Kerr, (aka the 'Galloping Gourmet') ran around the country telling saucy anecdotes and cooking up a storm.**

1970s

New tastes: Foreign dishes continued to grow in popularity. Ready-made foods flooded the market.

Favourite Catchphrase: 'It could make a dishonest woman of you (referring to how convincing and 'home cooked' convenience dishes appeared to be).

Sophisticated dishes: If you wanted to impress a date in the 1970s, you took her out for a meal of prawn cocktail, steak and chips and black-forest gateau (which is now making a comeback on retro menus).

Old Favourites: Fish and chips again! And custard – back in 1973, 16% of adults had custard at lunch.

Consumption: Large amounts of red meat were commonplace (almost double the current average person's weekly intake).

Hot in the kitchen: No-nonsense Delia Smith arrived with her straight-forward brand of cookery and advice, which has seen her popularity last over 35 years to date.

1980s

New tastes: A new interest in health meant low-fat pasta was the latest thing.

Favourite Catchphrase: 'Too much on the bill and not enough on the plate' (referring to nouvelle cuisine).

Sophisticated dishes: Nouvelle cuisine – tiny portions of intricately-prepared food, beautifully presented, that was surprisingly filling.

Consumption: Strangely enough, it was the decade that sales of both nouvelle cuisine, and hamburgers really took off! Work that one out!

Hot in the kitchen: One of the first foreign chefs to make an impact was Madhur Jaffray, ensuring our spice racks had more in them than just curry powder. Cooking Indian food at home became all the rage.

Robert only just resisted enquiring if there was a war.

1990s

New Tastes: Pre-washed bagged salads were introduced, containing unheard of ingredients like radiccio, rocket and lollo rosso. Cereal bars took off for those without time to eat breakfast.

Favourite Catchphrase: Pukka! (see Kitchen Gods below)

Sophisticated dishes: Thai proved a big hit in the 90s.

Old Favourites: Thirty years on from falling into the general category of 'foreign muck', Chicken Tikka Masala was named as 'restaurant dish of the year'. Consumption: Much more fresh fruit and veg – lots of foreign, imported new tastes.

Kitchen Gods and Sirens: Jamie Oliver sprung onto the scene with his youthful enthusiasm, laddish approach and pukka catchphrase. Not to mention his own TV show and range of foods at Sainsbury's.

And into the 2000s.....

- Food allergies and intolerances now play a major part in life with lactose intolerance, wheat allergies and nut allergies being the most prevalent.

- Gordon Ramsay is at the peak of fame with Hell's Kitchen, Ramsay's Kitchen Nightmares, The 'F' Word, bad language and hatred of vegetarians.

- Nigella Lawson controversially refers to her offerings as 'gastro-porn'.

- Jamie Oliver revolutionises school dinners with his campaign for healthy eating and to end the reign of the Turkey Twizzler.

- Ethical and environmental eating is huge news. Food miles are counted across the length and breadth of Britain – at least in the home counties.

- Sales of pre-packed but health-conscious gastro meals are at an all-time high.

And beyond...New Food Buzzwords

Things to look out for...

Bio piracy: a term coined by charity Action Aid to describe how large companies hijack basic foods by making small alterations to and then patenting them (i.e. basmati rice)

Cholesterol-free: much-loved term used to promote sales of margarines and spreads.

Environmental eating: encompassing fair trade, sustainability and food miles.

Food coma: slang term for the lethargic state induced by overindulgence in carbohydrate-laden food.

Live Food: raw food in its natural state where nothing has been lost in the cooking process.

Performance-boosting: a term loved by manufacturers who claim consuming their products will improve all-round performance.

Phytochemicals: natural chemicals in plants that claim health benefits. Heavily pushed by brands that promote 'healthier' foods.

Retro eating: eating that evokes a sentimental, rose-tinted memory of times gone by. Especially popular with the baby-boomer generation.

Snack pimping: home cookery where the chef creates giant versions of an original snack product (i.e. Jaffa Cakes or muffins).

Wild-caught: favourite term on menus in the mid-2000s. Alludes to the fact the fish or meat has not been factory-farmed.

How Nigel hated the pea-dilemma.
Testosterone versus table manners.

How Not To Cause Offence
Around The World:

Afghanistan
Guests always refrain from eating too much, unless the host coaxes them to eat more. Even then the host should always ask at least three times if the guest wants more food and the guest should politely decline at least three times before accepting. In certain situations the host can put food on the guest's plate by force.

Canada
Inuit people in Canada indicate their enjoyment at the end of a meal by belching.

In China it is considered rude to clear your plate, as it indicates that you are still hungry.

Also, never stab chopsticks into a bowl of rice, leaving them standing upwards. Any stick-like object facing upward resembles the incense sticks that some Asians use as offerings to deceased family members. This is considered the ultimate faux pas on the dining table.

France

Both hands must be above the table at the same time. They cannot be below the table even if they are together.

Phillipe could never resist a quick fiddle with his baguette between courses.

India

You should maintain absolute silence while taking food. You are not expected chat unnecessarily with the people around the table.

The cardinal rule of dining is to always use the right hand when eating or receiving food and never the left, as it is considered unclean.

Japan

Loud slurping whilst eating udon, ramen or soba noodles is perfectly acceptable. The Japanese maintain that inhaling air when eating hot noodles improves the flavor.

Mexico

It is not acceptable to pass gas at the table, unless only drunk men are present.

Phillipines

Don't talk about world destruction at the dinner table.

Spain

In Spain restaurant diners may brush their crumbs and wrappers onto the floor at the end of a meal, where everything will be swept up at the end of the day.

When the upper classes used to dine, they would often use code around the table to highlight a problem. If anyone uttered FHB, that would mean the hostess did not think there was enough to go round, and was instructing that 'family hold back' from the food.

Another popular one was to enquire 'have you written to mother?' which would indicate to the recipient that they were holding their cutlery incorrectly.

Food Snobbery Checklist
Pretentious? Moi?

Chances are you may be somewhat of a snob if:

- You question other people's choices in a restaurant. And then bring it up again later.

- You notice the absence of garnish on a plate.

- You sit watching someone preparing food, and cannot help interjecting and then taking over, as you know you do it better.

- Anything pre-packaged is the devil's work, according to your good self.

- You gleefully pat yourself on the back when the latest food scare or food contamination report comes out. As you do not buy pre-packaged or anything less than organic, it just won't affect you.

- You call everything by its French name. Or you correct everyone's pronunciation around the table when they try to call it by its French name.

- You purposely fill your pantry with ingredients that are hard to find, unpronounceable or inedible, just to impress people.

- You make the same dinner for a friend that they made you once, just to show how it really can look and taste.

- You have, at some time said to your partner 'you're not going to present it looking like that, are you?'

- If you talk about the cooking process using professional terminology ad hoc, just to confuse your guests, then you're probably one.

- And likewise, if you keep a collection of knives that cost more than your recent extension, that's a clue. Nobody needs ever-sharp bespoke knives, counter and weight balanced, designed exclusively to fit their hand.

But take heart, there are plenty of you out there. According to a feature in The Observer Food Monthly, amongst the top 50 things recommended for foodies to do before they die, are (in no particular order):

- Learn how to make a perfect Martini (which happens to be six parts gin to one part Vermouth)

- Tread grapes in a laga

- Buy a turbot (obviously, fresh from the boat and preferably served with a little Hollandaise sauce)

- Poach a snail (as in the cooking method, not nicking it when nobody's looking)

- Visit Highgrove, to see first-hand how a bottomless pit of money can provide best-practice organic farming

- Milk a cow

- Queue for fish and chips (they recommend Aldeburgh fish and chip shop in Suffolk)

- Pod fresh peas (something all working-class women did as a matter of course in the 30s – usually on their front doorstep)

- Try Japanese Blowfish – (and just hope its been prepared by a chef who knows what he's doing!)

- Be cooked for by a legend

- Get up early and go to market

Food snobbery stories:

The fad for mixing ridiculous ingredients to appeal to ever-more demanding palates reached its zenith when snail porridge, and smoked bacon and egg ice cream joined the menu at the Fat Duck at Bray. Award-winning chef Heston Blumenthal, referring to some of his other offerings, said "Eat sardine on toast sorbet for the first time and confusion will reign as the brain will be trying to tell the palate to expect a dessert and you will therefore be tasting more sweetness than actually exists."

You're not a food snob if your reaction to that is 'who could be arsed? I'd rather have food my brain and stomach can recognise instantly'.

Back in the 1960s, the health and hygiene restrictions we have today were nowhere to be seen, so it's possible to see how pub landlord Malcolm Moyer got away with selling bottles of his famous wine L'eau Duponde for five months. Described as 'matured locally. A heady wine, varying in colour with a unique bouquet. It should be drunk with a pinch of salt', the 'wine' was actually duck pond water, placed on the wine list as a trap for wine snobs. Mr Moyer was delighted to have caught over 50 of them in the time it was served.

A very popular starter at Birmingham's Ipanema restaurant during my time as general manager was the Asparagus Tips with a Hollandaise Sauce. There were countless people that ate the root of the asparagus and left the tips – but the best bit was when they would then go on to drink the finger bowl!

– Phil Lunn, Birmingham

Wine Trivia

Wine should be stored on its side to keep the cork from drying out.

As a rule of thumb, it takes approximately 2.4lbs grapes to make one bottle of wine.

Napa Valley recently surpassed Disneyland as America's number one attraction, with an annual 5.5 million visitors.

The 5 Minute Wine Course

Wines are available in three types: red, white and rosé.

The 'vintage' is the year the wine was made and is shown on the label of the bottle. The older the wine the more mature, and, in theory, better.

If a wine is referred to as 'corked' it means it has been tainted by a bad cork during the ageing process and may have bits of cork in it and probably won't taste as it should.

As a rule European wines are named after the regions from which they originate: (i.e. Bordeaux, Champagne). New World wines tend to be named after the grape variety used to make them.

Chill red wine for 5 minutes and white for 20 minutes before serving.

Tips from a real wine waiter:
(courtesy of www.waiterrant.net)

- DO NOT SMELL THE CORK! – When I see someone do this I know I'm dealing with a complete amateur. Guess what you'll smell? Cork!

- You should feel the cork to make sure it's intact. Is the bottom of the cork moistened with wine? Good. That means it was stored properly.

- Make sure the name on the cork matches the name on the bottle. Sometimes unscrupulous bastards put cheap wine in old wine bottles and re-cork them! Is there mould on the cork? That's a bad sign.

- Don't forget smelling the cork, in the vast majority of cases, tells you nothing. (Full disclosure: I used to smell the cork before I was a waiter.)

- AND DON'T SMELL THE PLASTIC CORK EITHER! I can't tell you how many times I've seen people do this. Lots of wine makers are moving away from natural cork to synthetics. Sniffing a plastic cork tells the world you're a moron.

Did you know that peanuts are used in the manufacture of dynamite?

General Food Facts

- Canned rattlesnake meat first went on sale in America in 1931.

- The average prisoner in the Second World War death camps was given around 1,300 calories per day. This is more than many dieters consume on modern-day diets.

~ source: Paul McKenna (I
Can Make You Thin)

- A single Alaskan Crab can have up to a 6 inch leg span and yield over 6 lbs of meat.

- Eskimos use refrigerators to keep food from freezing.

- White Castle was the world's first hamburger chain, founded in 1921 in Wichita Kansas.

- It takes 3,500 surplus calories to make a pound of body fat.

- The average human runs on a similar amount of energy required to power a 100 watt lightbulb.

- Approximately 815 million people in the world are under-nourished today. And thanks to excess consumption of junk and fast-food, that includes developed countries too.

- The poultry industry's huge loss per year on cracked eggs is because some hens stand on tiptoe to lay – and consequently their eggs drop harder onto the floor.

- A rye plant puts out 3 miles of roots in a day!

- The Chinese prefer black-haired dog meat, to white-haired dog meat.

Marketing & Advertising Facts

- Fifty six companies are involved in getting one can of chicken noodle soup onto supermarket shelves.

- Although hunger in a world of plenty is a tale as old as time, the contrast has seldom been demonstrated more graphically than it was in 1985. While the American administration sent $500 million to help save the lives of the wasted skeletons of Ethiopia, Americans themselves spent $5,000 million on trying to lose weight.

- In 2001 £181.3m was spent on alcohol advertising.

- Women are seen as key to chocolate advertising, as they are the gatekeepers to the rest of the family.

- 'My Fruit Is Bloody Lovely' – sign on side of fruit van, seen in Corfu.

Disgusting Facts

- Every portion of water you drink has already been drunk by someone else, possibly several times over.

- FDA Government guidelines (no. 20) indicate 'an average of two rodent hairs per one hundred grams of peanut butter is allowed'

- Scottish housewife Jill Martin laced her husband's curry with dog faeces after enduring five years of mental cruelty.

- Did you know that Milk containing up to 400 million pus cells per litre may be legally sold for human consumption! That means that one teaspoon of milk could contain 2 million pus cells.

- An Austrian doctor has advocated the practice of nose-picking and eating the contents, saying it's 'the perfect way for the body to build up its immune system'

THE LICK OF LUXURY

The chocolate was just like a man.... it lured her in with promises of happiness, but was much more pleasant to swallow.

Luscious Chocolate Trivia

A plethora of luscious facts for the chocoholic

• Allergies to chocolate are very uncommon.

• Contrary to popular myth, chocolate is NOT responsible for causing headaches. They are far more likely to be caused by either hunger, sleep deprivation or dehydration.

• Switzerland consumes the most chocolate per year per head of population.

• The chocolate advertising market is worth over £5 billion per year worldwide.

• The coca plant grows up to 20 to 25 feet tall.

• M&Ms were first created for the US military, as their shells prevented them from melting.

• In 1657 the first chocolate shop opened in London. Prior to that, only nobility could drink it.

• Three lanes of a highway in Sao Paolo, Brazil were once covered in chocolate when a tanker overturned and lost its contents. Children materialised from all over the place, and rolled around in the chocolate, refusing to get up. Police described it as: 'the best accident ever'.

Chocolate And Sex

According to Murray Langham, a New Zealand-born psychotherapist and author of the book 'Chocolate Therapy: Dare To Discover Your Inner Self', much of a person's personality traits can be revealed by their choice of a chocolate's shape and filling.

In his observations he noted that:

• Lovers of milk chocolate tend to be innocent people who like to live in the past.

• Lovers of dark chocolate are materialistic, problem solvers, who are excited by the future.

• Lovers of white chocolate are afficianados, who have an innate sense of fairness and believe they have the power of the universe at their command.

By observing chocolate eaters' habits he noted that:

• The filling and shape of a person's choice of chocolate reveals much about their personality and state of mind.

• Lovers of oval-shaped chocolates, for instance, are social and sensual.

• Those who prefer a coffee filling are open-minded, but also impatient, anxious and immature.

• He could discover more about their personalities and beliefs than by asking straightforward questions.

Even attitudes to sex are revealed:

• He concluded that those people who crinkle the wrapping before throwing it away tend to have too many thoughts on their mind and are unable to concentrate in bed.

• People who roll the paper into a ball, on the other hand, are having a very boring sex life.

And it's not just him:

• In April 2007 the Daily Telegraph reported that new research showed eating chocolate to be more stimulating than passionate kissing, with the intense buzz and pleasure experienced lasting up to four times longer thann the effects of a kiss!

• In a study of 163 Italian women, researchers found that those consuming chocolate on a daily basis had higher levels of desire than those who did not, thus concluding that chocolate has a positive physiological impact on a woman's sexuality.

Hurrah!!

Chocolate Quotes

There are four basic food groups: milk chocolate, dark chocolate, white chocolate and chocolate truffles.

~ Anon

Strength is the capacity to break a chocolate bar in four pieces with your bare hands and just eat one piece.

~ Judith Vorst

The 12-step chocoholics programme - NEVER BE MORE THAN 12 STEPS FROM CHOCOLATE!

~ Terry Moore

Man: Is that all you've got to eat?
Waiter: No sir. I'll be having a nice shepherd's pie
when I get home!

If you're dining with us, there are a few things you may like to know...

Enjoy our food 'served in style, all on dish reminiscent of the minge dynasty'

~ Cantonese restaurant menu

Customers who consider our waitresses uncivil should see the manager.

~ Notice in café

Attention – use of mobile phone may affect the quality of our food.

– Restaurant in Venice

Is forbidden to steal hotel cutlery please. If you are not such person to do such is please not to read notis.

– Tokyo hotel

It is not considered polite to tear bits off your beard and put them in your soup.

~ 1930s notice in actor's lodgings

Service by fancy boys and girls.

~ Japanese hotel advert

The noodles is not our best dish, but is by far cheapest.

~ Notice in Yorkshire budget café

Who cares if the customer is always right?

True bad service stories

I was in a really nice downtown restaurant, when our waiter farted really loudly, whilst reciting the specials. And then he carried on as if nothing had happened. Was that really gross service, or really great aplomb?

~ Esther, New York

I once went to a restaurant where the food was so bad it was incredible. The pudding was the worst of the lot though, when the 'Tower of Fresh Summer Fruits' turned out to be tinned Morello cherries, that tasted of aluminium and were so old they were fermenting. I called the Maitre'D over again and explained there was no way we were going to pay, as the whole meal was so bad. He got very aggressive, but just before it turned into a fight, my friend very helpfully threw up (too much hysterical laughing and bad food). Suddenly desperate to get us out, we were shown the door and the situation was over.

We still laugh about it now.

~ Liz L, Birmingham

I was once dining out, when the waiter cracked a joke, laughed hysterically and then lost his tongue piercing. In my food.

~ Anon

I was with the office party one Christmas, and asked for my meat well done. It came to the table blue. I sent it back and asked for it well done, but it returned pink. In exasperation, I explained to the waitress that I'm from the North, and like my meat well-cooked. She came back, looking very embarrassed, and said 'the chef says if you want your meat burned then go to McDonalds.'

~ Ruth, Birmingham
(experienced at The Chiswick, Chiswick High Road – 1998)

You notice how shallow people are when you have a famous friend. My best mate is a film producer. You would be amazed how many times unsolicited film scripts have landed in his lap somewhere between courses. But the worst time was the waiter who presented the script before starters, and kept coming back to ask him if he'd read it. A total nightmare!

– William, Los Angeles

There's an Italian Restaurant in town that used to be very popular with footballers. In its heyday it was packed, and I think the staff got a little big for their boots. I've been on several occasions, and observed two things. One, is that they always, but always, seemed to make a mistake with the drinks bill. The second was the standard of service. One time, we were asked to move to make way for another table (we hadn't finished pudding), but the main time was when I called the waiter to say that my meat was overdone. He grabbed the knife and fork out of my hand, and started cutting up the meat into little pieces, shouting that there was nothing wrong with it – it was fine! I just sat there with a stunned look on my face, wanting to push his face into the plate. And I've never gone back there again.

~ **Ali, Birmingham** (of
San Carlo, Birmingham – 2003)

My friend and I decided to go to the Green Room café for Sunday lunch. We arrived at 1.30 and ordered drinks and then began to peruse the menu. We decided to stick to the set Sunday lunch. We waited awhile and eventually ordered another round of drinks from the bar. When no-one still came to take our order I waved frantically to one of the waitresses and she grinned and waved back enthusiastically. Eventually I had to go to the counter and ask if we could be served. The waitress I had waved at then came over to take the order. We said we would both like the set Sunday lunch. She informed us they only served that until 3.00 and we would now have to order from the main menu. I didn't like to point out that we had been sitting there for almost 2 hours so we waved at her again .... as we left without ordering.

~ Gareth A, Birmingham

MAY I TAKE YOUR ORDER?

Hilarious menu translations

All of the following are genuine translations from cafés, hotels and restaurants from around the world.

China
- Dreaded Veal Cutlet in cream
- We serve dead shrimp on vegetables with a smile
- Domestic life beef immerses cabbage
- Benumbed hot huang fries belly silk

England
- Beasts Of The Local Field
- Crap Cakes
- Profitter Rolls

France
- Raped carrots
- Alcohol and stranger wines

Greece
- Lamb chops
- Hogs shops
- Salad of a village
- Cuntry salad

India
- Chicken Football
- Chicken Cock roll
- Three cute prawns suntanning on the rice
- Deep fried fingers of my lady
- Stuffed nun among the breads

Istanbul
- Meat in gobbets
- Chicken Nutts

Mexico
- Potatoes fried to the French

Poland
- Roasted duck let loose

Prague
- A strawberry mirror (which had been translated from the french 'fromage au glacé')

Switzerland
- Our wines leave you nothing to hope for
- Special today – no ice cream

Tanzania
- Staff at the Ngorongoro lodge in Tanzania were rendered helpless with laughter and unable to work by their English manager's mistake, when she advertised Kuma for lunch. In Swahili kumi is 10, whereas Kuma is actually the word for vagina.

Turkey

(This was a complete menu, which so many tourists apparently stopped to laugh at, a huge crowd gathered and the owner was busy all day!)

- Grill in due form of Anatolia
- Spit
- Special Spit from our kitchen
- Chepherd Spit
- Schnitzel
- Beefsteak
- Hen Spit

Vietnam
- Pork with fresh garbage

HOME COOKING

Just like mother used to make.

Packaging - Instructions and Warnings:

On a ketchup bottle:
Instructions - Put on food.

This packet of ready-made pastry will be enough for four persons or 12 tarts.

On a bag of Fritos:
You could be a winner! No purchase necessary. Details inside.

Printed on the bottom of Tesco Tiramisu dessert:
Do not turn upside down.

On a muffin packet:
Remove wrapper, open mouth, insert muffin, eat.

On Marks and Spencer Bread Pudding:
Product will be hot after heating.

On Sainsbury's peanuts:
Warning: Contains nuts.

On the bottom of a cola bottle:
Do not open here.

On an American Airlines packet of nuts:
Instructions: open packet, eat nuts.

Fast food outlet warning on cup of coffee:
Caution. Contents may be hot.

Real warning on beer:
Consumption of alcohol may lead you to believe that ex-lovers are really dying for you to telephone them at 4 in the morning.

IMPORTANT: Albadoro Cannelloni – do not ought to boil

1) Bring in Cannelloni, as they are, a stuffing maked with beef, eggs, cheese parmigian, papper or spices, as you like, all well amalgamated ad juicy.

2) Besmear a backing-pan, previously buttered with a good tomato sauce and after, dispose the Cannelloni lightly distanced between them, in an only couch.

3) At last, for a safe success in cooking, shed the remnant sauce, possibly diluted with broth, as far as to cover the surface of Cannelloni.

4) Add puffs of butter and grated cheese, cover the backing-pan, and put her into the oven, previously warmed at 180/200 centigrade degrees above zero.

5) Cook for about an half of hour at the same temperature without to uncover the backin-pan and after, to help at table.

True stories:

Floating on air, I hastily grabbed ingredients from the shelf in my rather dubious local shop. I had bagged my man, secured that all important first intimate date, and in my heady state was planning an intimate meal for two cooked by my own fair hand! I was 18, and had never done much more than supernoodles and Cornflakes, so was really excited to be doing a full roast, thinking no doubt he'd fall head over heels in love with me.

The chicken I settled on (the only one left on the shelf) did seem to have a slightly yellowish tinge and rather a peculiar odour but, flushed with excitement, I brushed any doubts aside, and soon it was browning in the oven.

When my potential new love arrived, he was suitably impressed. My flat was aglow with tea lights, Nina Simone was playing softly in the background and the aroma of roast chicken completed the ambience.

With seduction in mind, I opened some wine, beckoned him to the table and ran to get the chicken. Once we were both seated, I began spooning the veg, while he began to carve the bird.

He didn't notice at first – neither did I (we were both a bit tipsy and I was just thinking of the snog to come). But then came his ear-splitting shriek and a trail of obscenities. And then he knocked over the wine in his desperation to get away from the table.

I followed its watery trail across the tablecloth in my shocked state and then I saw – the cloth was alive! Moving, squirming.......hundreds of wriggling, maggots, teeming from the remains of the chicken in their haste to escape the heat of my wonderful dinner. They were all over the plates, the table, the veg – and us!

In the uproar and hurling of abuse, I noted the table had been upturned, then heard the slamming of the door. Only then did I snap back from the shock that had rooted me and I ran after him. But I never made it to the door. I tripped on broken plates and lay in the maggoty carnage, stunned, irrationally wondering if he'd have enjoyed my home made trifle a bit more!

~ Kerry Olson, Southend

At my first informal dinner party a few years ago, I just had a few guests and my parents in attendance.

Because I spent so much time on the main course, I wimped out on dessert, and just brought out a kiwi fruit, and a knife for each one of them. I half noticed my dad eying his plate suspiciously, then seconds later he picked up his kiwi and biting into it like an apple announced to the room … "lovely…. it's just like a hairy gooseberry"…

~ Darren Hodson, Birmingham

I had guests over for dinner and drinks, and it all seemed to be going very well until I made G&Ts for everyone. We'd all clinked glasses and taken our first sip, when everyone simultaneously choked, gargled or went 'Uurgh' and spat it out.

It tasted vile – horribly salty and a bit fishy. It was then I realised I'd used frozen vegetable stock cubes by mistake. How we laughed. Just!

~ Carrie, Belfast

Tinned corned beef is a useful reserve of meat for the household. It is minced beef, cast in a block with hard beef fat.

I prefer it without the fat. I make a pad of about eight layers of kitchen paper towelling and put the corned beef and pad under the grill. When the block has softened I spread the meat over the pad. The heat melts the fat, which soaks into the pad, like blotting paper.

After use, the pad is discarded. By the next day, when the fat has hardened again, the pad is astonishingly hard and stiff.

– letter in the Sutton Coldfield News

I confess. I regularly buy cheese-topped bread rolls and eat only the cheese. I throw away the bread. I have contemplated melting more cheese on the cheese-less left over, dough, letting it cool and go crispy and picking it off all over again. I could repeat this exercise using the same bread roll over and over again. It's genius.

- from a poster on Gumtree website

THE ESTABLISHMENT STRIKES BACK

Wayne paid back his difficult customers with extra 'powdered milk' in their coffee.

Staff Confessions

This is a vile admission. I worked at a filthy restaurant called Muswells, back in the 80s. It's closed down now – thank God. It was so bad, I eventually called in the specialists to do what's called a 'deep clean'. It became apparent how bad it was, when one of the guys came in to tell me he'd found a rat in the corner of the restaurant – being sick!

~ Sarah Goody, London

I had to make an emergency coffee for a diner. We had run out of fresh coffee, so it had to be instant. I put in a spoon of Coffee Mate and ran to the table, only to see by the time I got there it was full of hideous lumps. It turned out that I'd actually put in instant potato. The diner was not impressed.

~ Jan, Coleshill, West Midlands

I was working at a top Midlands hotel where all the stars stay, and we had a very, very famous guest who wanted tomato soup at 3 am. We had nothing to offer, so I raced out to the local Tesco and got a tin of Heinz tomato, heated it in the microwave, and charged him £11.50 for it.

~ Anon, New Hall Hotel, 2002

I can't help it. I always lick the teaspoon before serving coffee.

~ Anon, New York

I hate it when people read the full description off the menu. Instead of taking two minutes to run through the whole description, why can't they just point and say 'I'll have the cod'?

- Mark, Somerset

I work at the Ivy in London, and there's some idiot that comes in with business colleagues, and always makes a point of ordering off-menu. I wouldn't mind, but all the dickhead ever wants is ham and chips.

- Anon

I worked in tons of different places when I was a trainee chef, and I can tell you that the 'rumours' that you hear about mistreatment of food are absolutely true. In one restaurant, I saw the same chef wipe a steak around a toilet bowl and then flash-cook it in the pan. I even saw him pee into a risotto. I barely ever eat out now.

— Liz L, Birmingham

Part of being on a placement usually means being treated horribly as part of the initiation. It happens a lot in hotels and restaurants and top 'tricks' played on me included:

- being given tweezers and told to 'fillet' the anchovies
- make tartan food colouring
- go to the wholesalers and collect a 'longwaite'

I also had to peel and bottle 20lbs of garlic in oil once. I smelled so bad, that I couldn't even have my chef's whites in the bedroom with me.

– Lucy Baker, Frinton

Whilst working as a 'silver service' waiter at Birmingham's world famous N.E.C. the guest of honour at one particular function was H.R.H. Princess Michael of Kent. As a typical gay man I'm easily impressed by royalty, glamour and jewellery, so a combination of nerves and awe lead to me dropping a small potato into the lap of H.R.H. ...

She looked up at me with horror, but suddenly my gay wit returned, and I can't believe I actually said: 'It's alright duck -it's a Jersey Royal!"

~ Luscious, Birmingham

Management Confessions

I run a catering company, and people would be amazed to know what goes on behind the scenes. In an effort to steal my business, competitors have tried lots of different methods, including calling and offering huge incentives like £15k worth of kitchen equipment to change from my company to theirs, ringing competitors to tell them I have gone out of business and am about to be liquidated, and the worst one – my opposition waited until I went on holiday, and then rang up one of my contracts saying I'd been killed in a car crash, and they could 'come in immediately and take over – just to ensure nobody is aware'! It was disgraceful.

– Anon

My husband and I used to run a hotel, and one Christmas we had in a local womens' Christian group. They were lovely to start with, all chatting away – a very vibrant buzz around the room, but as the starters were served, we could hear the sound of spoons hitting plates, conversation running dry, and then silence. It was terrifying – we were all hidden behind the kitchen door, like something out of Fawlty Towers, fighting over who was going to go out and face them. Suddenly, these lovely ladies had turned into harridans because their soup was burned! Well – we took the bowls away and served them melon (that we were going to bin as it had gone soft), so that saved the day. But then the turkey was very tough, and the silence dropped again. We ended up plying them with drink and giving every meal away for free. We lost around £3,000 that lunchtime and we left catering shortly afterwards. They were the scariest women I've ever met!

– Sue, Birmingham

I have long since left catering, but still feel bad about deducting staff's tips from their wage packets. And making passes at the younger ones. And bouncing cheques on them. I just hope they've got better bosses now.

~ Dean, Weymouth

Michelin's Eh? Eh? Guide To The World's Worst Restaurants

The size of the pudding could not be estimated, as three quarters of it was missing.

– Comment on visitor's book in private hotel

The service gently unravelled – and then less gently. It was like watching someone's knitted skirt catch on a nail and leave them standing in bra and panties. They ran out of cutlery, then patience, then any clue and the will to live, but remained surprisingly charming and, if not helpful, then helplessly optimistic. I particularly liked the girl whom I finally begged to give me a bill. She had plainly decided to rise above all of this.

– review of Inn the Park (Alex James, Sunday Times)

I sometimes feel that more lousy dishes are presented under the banner of pâté than any other."

~ **Kingsley Amis**

Tamarind, a Michelin-starred Indian restaurant in London? It looked like a works canteen in Hull. Not that I've ever been to Hull or to a works canteen.

~ **Michael Winner**
(November 2003)

Spoon, Sanderson hotel, London: the restaurant is hideous. The food was absolutely terrible. I finished with a dessert that almost defies description, but I'll manage. It was called Nutella tart. It tasted as if it had sat on a railway-station buffet for weeks.

– Michael Winner
(March 2001)

Why the security guards? And lastly, why watermelon in a plastic tub for £4.55. Is it hand-cut by a disabled person somewhere in a remote village?

– **Dissatisfied customer** (at Whole Foods, Kensington, London)

Apparently, Beau Brummel was dining at a household in Hampshire where he found the champagne to be decidedly inferior. History has it that he waited for a lull in the conversation before calling loudly to the wine servant, 'John, give me some more of that cider will you.'

Crap, but my friends Nick and Jim bought me here.

~ **Another customer**
(at Whole Foods, Kensington, London)

This place makes me want to saw off my foot, just to slap the staff out of their minimalist trance.

~ **Giles Coren** (on
Yauatcha, London)

Why Not Toss Over Your Favourite Food?

The joy of badly researched product names

(with many thanks for input to www.dazbert.co.uk)

Alcohol

- Who would have thought that in Norway, they enjoy a bottle of Aass beer every now and then? But probably not as much as the Irish enjoy the pubicly-angled Black Bush Irish Whisky. However, in the USA, they prefer to be refreshed by a beverage known as Wanker Beer – a top seller no doubt... if you can get your hands on it!

- But what better way to finish off all this liquid innuendo, than with a bottle of Dry Sack – a medium/dry sherry that contains no warnings whatsoever about its ability to sap a man of his last droplets, but does claim to satisfy 'the most demanding palates'. Oh well – there's some compensation.

- When it comes to snacks and sweeties, the world really is your oyster. While the ever-modest Belgians munch on Big Nuts chocolate bars, the French prefer their chocolate known as Crap's. In Sweden, Finger Marie isn't an instruction, but a thin biscuit made by McVities – who surely must be having a laugh?

- And on the subject of biscuits – has anyone enjoyed Coming lately? This delightful name belongs to a Japanes candy biscuit type product, where it's also available as Coming lemon. Those naughty Japanese are also behind the Creamy Collon – little tubes of packed full of creamy white confection – (which all sounds a tad specialist for most of us).

- And if the Creamy Collon needs a bit of releasing – you could always resort to a good old Familie Guf. In Swedish, Guf actually means sweets, but in order to keep the theme going, we like to imagine a broad-minded Swedish family, all getting together with their chunky sweaters on for a good old fart. So bonding!

Soft Drinks

- There seems to be an obsession with the nether regions in the drink department, starting with those open-minded Swedes who get their energy from a drink called Erektus.

- In Germany a well-established brand of lemonade is called, onomatopaeically, 'Psschitt!' Combine this with the German word for bottle and you can happily pop into a local supermarket and ask for 'eine flasche Psschitt! Bitte.'

- The Germans actually prefer Prick Cola, whilst the Polish regularly enjoy a bottle of Fart juice. However, the Mexicans top the lot by guzzling down gallons of a drink enticingly named 'Ice Cold Poop'.

Snacks
- Grated Fanny tuna probably isn't everyone's dream meal, but it seems to go down well in Aruba in the Caribbean. It's also possible to get Cock Soup in Jamaica, and something called Tiny Tit Bits in Eastern Europe. However, things get a bit larger in Indonesia with Super Titi 33, which must surely be a prelude to the Bimbo Sandwich, available in Barcelona?

- At one stage, Wimpey were offering the delightful Chicken Bender (also available as a 'bender in a bun' version). For those less-enlightened readers, bender is another name for a homosexual man – surely a marketing faux pas, if ever there was one? But even more so, when you consider that a 'chicken', is the gay name for an underage boy!

- If you happen to find yourself in France, Cok Bacon crisps are extremely popular, as is Happy Crak! popcorn in Spain. But to top it all, you'd have to go to Australia to experience probably the most provocative ice cream/biscuit combo known as 'Gaytime'. Even funnier was the original advertising campaign, that allegedly featured people sneaking off to selfishly eat their Gaytime, only to be intruded upon, with the voiceover claiming 'It's so hard to have a Gaytime on your own'...!

Basics
- Fancy a sarni (sandwich)? Well why not spread your farmhouse bap with a liberal application of Botteram? Sounding like something to do with hard anal sex, it's actually a vegetable spread found in Greece. However, we assume it could possibly double up, if you find yourself in a remake of Last Tango In Paris.

- Or alternatively, you could spread your Botteram all over some Jussipussi. These fabulous doughy rolls are available in Finland, although they don't look quite as moist and promising as their name suggests.

MISCELLANEOUS

Did you know, there's an International Federation of Competitive Eating?

Here, members are known as 'gustatory athletes '(or epicurians in French). They are advised not to 'train' alone at home as it may be dangerous.

Current records include

Butter:
7 quarter-pound sticks, salted butter: 5 minutes: Don Lerman

Cow Brains:
57 (17.7 pounds): 15 minutes: Takeru Kobayashi

Hamburgers:
11 1/4 pound "Cloud Burgers" in 10 minutes: Don Lerman

Chicken Nuggets:
80 in 5 minutes: Sonya Thomas

Glazed Doughnuts:
49 in 8 minutes: Eric Booker

Food Questions

Dear Sirs
When purchasing your biscuits, I cannot help but notice that the top biscuit is nearly always broken. May I suggest that in future, you should leave out the top biscuit in each pack?

~ N Jackson, letter to manufacturer

Q: Do ham and iced tea taken at the same time create a liquid in the stomach similar to ink?

A: I know of no scientific or dietetic reason why this would happen.

~ letter in Good Housekeeping magazine

If toast always lands butter-side down, and cats always land on their feet, what happens if you strap toast on the back of a cat and drop it?"

~ Steven Wright

Foodie Jokes

- What's the difference between a culinary snob and a soufflé?
  One is puffed up and full of hot air, the other you can eat.

- What's the difference between Gordon Ramsay and a cross country runner?
  One's a pant in the country.

- The Pillsbury Doughboy died yesterday of a yeast infection and trauma complications from repeated pokes in the belly. He was 71.

- Practice safe eating. Always use condiments

RESOURCES

If you are interested in any aspect of food, why not check out the following organisations and resources, which proved helpful in the compilation of this book.

Alcohol Concern

The Food Standards Agency

Social Issues Research Centre, Oxford

The International Federation of Competitive Eating

The Vegetarian and Vegan Foundation

www.chocolate.org.uk

www.chocholate.co.uk

www.cockeyed.com

www.dazbert.co.uk

www.doheth.co.uk

www.echomouse.blogspot.com

www.eatwell.gov.uk

www.euromonitor.com

www.foodreference.com

www.gdargaud.net

www.nationalarchives.gov.uk

www.parliament.uk

www.rahoi.com

www.turkeytravelplanner.com

www.waiterrant.net

www.wikipedia.com